REAL WORLD 101: STUDENT GUIDE

REAL WORLD 101: STUDENT GUIDE

Alcott Germany II

CITI OF BOOKS

CITIOFBOOKS, INC.
3736 Eubank NE Suite A1
Albuquerque, NM 87111-3579
www.citiofbooks.com
Hotline: 1 (877) 389-2759
Fax: 1 (505) 930-7244

Ordering Information:
Quantity Sales. Special discounts are available on quantity purchases by corporations, associations, and others. For details, contact the publisher at the address above.

Printed in the United States of America.

ISBN-13   Paperback   978-1-960952-40-0
                      eBook   978-1-960952-41-7

Library of Congress Control Number: 2023910806

This book is dedicated to all those who taught me to believe in a better day.

Dear Parents,

Real World 101: Student Guide is a written discussion between the reader and the author on the topic of "the real world" and what that should mean to students who may currently just go through the motions of waking up and going to school. When students begin to see the repetition of school assignments, grades, and after-school activities, the motivation to continue on with achieving at a high level begins to fade. This is not at all different from the behavior shown by adults with repetitive tasks on the job. Students will see that the practical applications of school subjects are closely aligned to their own personal experience and interests. Seeing this relationship motivates students to maintain a high level of involvement inside and outside the classroom to learn about the world around them.

This student guide is broken into three parts: "What's this for?" "What now?" and "What next?" "What's this for?" is a dialog between the student and author that discusses the stereotypes of some of the more scrutinized subjects amongst students: mathematics, social studies, science, and the arts. These sections present to students the actual applications of these subjects as they tie into a student's world. When the dust is cleared about what these subjects look like to a student, the author and students journey on to explore the question of "What now?" Finally, they conclude with "What next?" which takes a quick look at the student game-plan beyond just the learning experience. Too many times students are provided with the message that scholastic achievement should be their primary focus, leaving them without means of understanding what all of this learning is leading them to know.

Ask yourself, what does victory even look like to an educated mind?

This book is designed to be a short and fun read for students that will allow them to develop an effective state of mind in understanding what it means to learn. What we want for our students is for them to have the skills needed to make effective decisions so that they can have control over their lives and not be too dependent on the success of past generations. Using this book, students will see that they are in a position to be more than capable of changing the real world for the better, but they must realize the real world scenarios they reside in now before these changes can occur.

Thank you for your time and support.

Sincerely,

Alcott Germany, II

Alcott Germany, II

Author

"When you achieve great things, people expect greatness. But no matter what others expect, the desire to succeed must come from yourself."

—Christa Rothenburger-Luding, East Germany
(Greenspan, 1997, p. 124)

Table Of Contents

THE STARTING POINT

Think back to your first school experience. You find yourself looking at new buildings, rooms, and hallways that look nothing like home. There are new adults, teachers and other school faculty overseeing you in the classroom and clearing the hallways, some of them resembling an adult relative you knew and others having just a strange look about them. More importantly of course, you are surrounded by an abundance of students your age to associate yourself with. Some of the students in the class you know from around the neighborhood, and others you have never seen before. You are motivated as a student because there are new things to do besides staying at someone's house and waiting for someone to get back home to keep you company. Homework is new (so it's not so bad now) and activities that are being done in the classroom are allowing you to learn new ideas that challenge you to learn basic concepts essential to life, such as learning to read, tell time, add, subtract, and eventually multiply and divide.

Some of you are even able to attend schools where art, music, and physical education are still primary elements of the curriculum. Remember finger painting exercises and crafts using paste made from flour and water that some students even considered eating? Wow! Some students were excited about recess (gym class), while others can remember picking up an instrument to play for the first time and beginning a new commitment to music and to the school band. At this time, school was new, students were new, extra-curricular activities were all new. Yeah, you could see yourself saying school is definitely the place to be!

Yet, as time progressed, assignments became repetitive; students would be asked to produce endless essays, projects, and presentations. School schedules expect students to attend school almost year-round. After a while you began to look forward to the winter breaks, spring breaks, fall breaks, and any other new break that could be invented. School started to be more of a chore rather than a fun learning experience. The "newness" of school that motivated you to go to school and made school fun for you and your peers is not so new anymore. The grades that are being used to test your skill level may or may not be where you want them to be, so the pressure to do well in school begins to affect your motivation as well. Your peers, who are not doing so well in school, begin to get distracted and look to other things to explore outside of the classroom so that they can get that feeling of "newness" back. Some of these activities are not positive and go against your upbringing, including drugs and violence. Later on, you look at your options and begin to ask yourself questions and make statements based on your situation, questions such as: "So why am I going to school anyway?" "What is all of this for?" "I know some people who are not doing so bad without it," and "Maybe this is not for me."

As you continue to read on, you will see that these are all questions that can be answered and statements that can be countered. It is also important to know that these are great questions that people, especially students, should ask. Let this book be a guide to help equip you with the truth, so that in the end you can counter all of these statements using your own words and thoughts. This read was not made to be long (this is not a textbook). The topics we discuss are intended to provide you with real-world topics that link what you see in the classroom to your surroundings and how that pertains to your own personal interests. Why do this? So you do not have to focus on what has already been done and relive the mistakes of the past. What society needs are new ideas for the future, things that have not been thought of or done before. Learning about the achievements and mistakes of the past is what will allow you to spend time on new ideas for the future, which means you get to focus on things that make you special. However, before this can happen, you need to learn the basics. Ready to get started? Good. Let's go.

WHAT'S THIS FOR?

Being able to see how your interests tie into the goals of academic achievement and the world around you (a.k.a. "the real world") starts with having a good understanding of what it is you are actually learning. What will these subjects do for you? Are these subjects only meant for certain people? When we are through, the final answer to both of these questions will come from you. When investigating the truth, the best sources are knowledgeable ones; teachers and even parents can help. Making decisions based on bad sources is similar to rumors you see spread in school (we know what those look like). So let's take a look at the truth about a couple of subjects. You will begin to find out that there are some real points as to why your educational journey is so important.

✐ *Mathematics*

As a student growing up, it was important for me to make a connection to the material so that I could succeed at an even higher level. In the classroom, you would hear me asking questions such as:

1. How does addition and subtraction help with multiplication and division?
2. How does knowing all that have to do with helping me with Algebra, Geometry, and Trigonometry?
3. How smart will I have to be to do this, and is Calculus even a possibility to learn?
4. Let's say I learn all of this math—then what?

You may think that these questions will get under someone's skin (namely a teacher or parent) and bother them, but questions such as these are all normal questions that should be asked. The importance behind asking these kinds of questions is that it allows you to formulate goals for yourself and a purpose for developing your skills in the subject. At some point you may have even heard your peers (including adults) say, "Why even excel in math after learning the basic functions (addition, subtraction, multiplication, division)?" "Don't we live in a society where money is most important? If we can add and subtract money, then that should be the end of where our skills need to go, right?"

Thinking in this way is what leads to underachieving efforts by students in the area of mathematics and especially in life. The truth about mathematics is that it is the study of logic, meaning that it is used to take a basic idea and connect it to something new through a series of steps. Basic logic is something that is exercised by people everyday. When getting dressed, eating, telling a story, trying to explain to your parents why your room is dirty or to your employer why you should get a raise, you must explain to them in a way that makes sense. Mathematics exercises your skills in how well you can prove a point in a way that makes sense.

Think about your life now. Even as students you are faced with challenges that need quick decisions and resolutions. The solutions that work best for you are the ones

Imagine one NBA team taking on all twenty-nine teams in the playoffs just to win a championship. Would you watch that?

that make sense, i.e., follow a logical sequence (Aha! There's that "logic" word again). Mathematics just uses numbers and symbols (x, y, z—seen these before?) in order to build your skills to problem solve. Do not let the "letters" from algebra shock or discourage you. The letters are just substitutes for numbers to show that regardless of the number chosen in a problem, the same result will continue to happen. Actually letters are used to make solving the situations or "equations" easier so you do not have to repeat the same sequence over again for every number (solving that way will take forever!). Think of a runner in a track meet who is a world record holder in a race. He or she is considered the fastest until their time is broken by another runner. Do you think it would be easier for that runner to run that race over and over again against every runner in the world to prove they are the fastest? Would an NBA basketball team play all twenty-nine teams in a seven-game series to prove they are the best? Not at all. If they did, the playoffs would be very long and very boring.

The same can be said about algebra and what letters are used for instead of numbers. They are actually used to reduce the amount of work needed in proving a point. Make sense? If so, then you just followed my logic!

Let's take this up a notch! Calculus has been looked upon by many students as a math subject that intimidates them. Do not let this happen to you. Calculus actually uses the basic concepts of algebra to solve the problems presented.

Just by using and making the connection to algebra, you can execute calculus problems at a very high achievement level.

Geometry uses rules of measurement and shapes (triangles, rectangles, and circles) to prove a point (deductive proofs). What you may not know is the same thought process that is used for these subjects is also used in the home, school, and even in a court of law. Think about a time when you had to prove a point to someone. You were actually using deductive reasoning as you would in geometry class. You were just replacing the facts about shapes with actual life events. Another example of a proof is a sales receipt from a restaurant. A receipt is a written proof to a customer showing the money needed to pay for food service. What if the bill is wrong? What if someone is wrong in the point they are trying to make on your behalf that you know cannot be true? When you do not take the initiative to prove your case and decide on others making decisions for you, the outcome in many situations will not result in your favor. Proving a point involves making sense out of what you believe, which is the same approach with solving problems in math on any level.

Understanding mathematical relationships and how they tie into the daily exchange of money is where you will grasp an understanding of how money is earned and spent. The different aspects of money (minimum wage, taxes, rent, and mortgage) have to do with statistics, which is more than just basic addition and subtraction. Statistics is important when learning how businesses function to stay open and grow into some of the major stores, movie theaters, restaurants, and other franchises you see today. So the next time you hear someone say that adding and subtracting is all that is needed in knowing about managing money, you now know how to respond.

What you have just read here are just a few examples of mathematics and the types of opportunities they provide in your development as a student. The main purpose for mathematics is to build problem-solving skills using numbers to present how ideas fit together. Your decision-making abilities will come to you quickly because you have exercised your problem-solving abilities in math class. Having problem-solving skills become second nature to you will lead to smart and effective decisions that will be based on your own judgment.

The point of this chapter is not to make everyone who reads it a calculus major or a professor. The intent is to ensure that as a student, you are not intimidated by challenges and misconceptions placed on mathematics causing you to miss out on numerous opportunities that will allow you to make positive changes for yourself and for others.

✐ Social Studies

A true fan favorite of every student's academic upbringing is social studies! Am I right? I actually recall discussing the American Revolution and the early Native Americans

"Is social studies all about land bridges and liberating the colonies from the British government?" "What are social studies and what are they about?"

crossing the land bridge in at least seven out of the first twelve years of school I had. Now, these were significant events in our country's history, but because of the repetition I began to miss out on the reason why this topic was important. Let us not forget the times where my class did get to cover the Civil War before school let out for the summer, so we did learn about the war against slavery and the fight for equal rights. You may not have had an experience like mine, but you still may wonder about the purpose of learning about all of these past moments that took place in our country. If these events happened in the past, what is the point of learning them? What do all of these events have to do with what is going on now?

Social studies may be the most important subject taught in our school system because social interactions and social behaviors occur daily. You see different social behaviors in the news, on the Internet and read about it in magazines everyday. The truth is that all of the social interactions and behaviors that we see today are based on the concepts found in social studies. Social studies provide lessons of the past and present in order for people to make "social" changes for the future.

What is pretty unique about social studies books is that new books with new information could really be released every year. Why? Because society continues to make historical changes every year. The decisions that we see made by elected officials (Presidents, senators, governors, and mayors) are all grounded in the history of social studies. Social studies can be rephrased easily as "the study of our society." Every aspect of American culture that you see and interact with on a daily basis is a reflection of our social culture. Musical breakthroughs (classical music, rock & roll, jazz, R&B, hip-hop), communication (the Internet, cell phones, email), even designer fashion are all examples of changes to the social environment that you see everyday. Speeches given by famous leaders and sports athletes setting records in various sports events are all significant historical events that are all a part of the subject of social studies.

Social studies exists closer to home than you may think at times. Taxes, school programs, and after-school programs are all examples of social studies that impact your life daily. There are many citizens that still live in your local neighborhoods today who served as pioneers—fighting against segregation, leading in innovation, and teaching truth, all resulting in changing the social culture of this country for the better.

"Why then," you ask, "are we to learn about land bridges and revolutions?" Quite simply, because the actions and decisions that you see made today are based upon the sacrifices, governing rules, and discoveries of yesterday. Learning from social events in the past led to positive changes, such as ending slavery, ending legal segregation, and providing every citizen equal rights to vote. Social studies show that life constantly changes, and rules to govern life should change with it for the good of the people. In other words, no law is etched in stone. This is why we have Amendments for Congress to constantly meet on so that laws will be made in an attempt to meet the social demands of the people. If change is what you want to make for those you care for and those you see in society (school, home, church, and job), it is important to first learn the events of the past and the rules of today. When studying social studies, understand the basic events of what happened in the past and see how these events connect to the present (sounds like math—remember logic?). Taking what you have learned and looking at ways to make changes you believe are needed in your environment is how "new rules" or laws are born. Making these "new rules" start with learning social studies. Now you know what it means when people ask, "What would you do if you were President?"

✐ *Science*

Now let us agree not to state the obvious. I could easily say that science will help you become a great doctor or engineer or some other job in the field of science.

Of course learning science is important for a career as a doctor! There are a lot more ways to use science that will allow you to make better decisions for yourself.

What if you do not have a dream of being a scientist (a mad scientist, as they used to say), engineer, archaeologist, or a doctor? What will science help with then?

Let us look at a typical scenario where science appears in our daily lives. Take for instance a visit to the hospital for you or your loved ones. In these facilities decisions are made by doctors and nurses to help fix ailments for others. Doctors and nurses are there to serve their patients, and a time may come when they will speak with you on health topics, procedures, and important life-changing decisions that they will want you to make. Comprehending what they have to say, asking questions, and knowing what parts of the body are being impacted describe the type of discussions you will want to have with them. They will do their best to answer any question you ask. However, many times the best answers only come from

Fuse boxes and power meters in your basement and backyard all function using electricity – a base concept of physics.

asking great questions. Having a basic understanding of the body (biology) and how other organisms and environments can impact it (life science—that's right!) will help in developing survival skills that will come in handy at some of the most amazing times. Prescription drugs in fighting diseases or symptoms of disease use terminology from chemistry. Physics is used in developing automobiles and for knowing how power companies charge for electrical usage and repair around your home.

I can guarantee you that most people with a ton of Christmas lights on their door (especially with musical effects) definitely used basic physics concepts to brighten up the streets.

These are just a couple of examples to wrap your mind around how this subject lives around you everyday and to show you that contrary to popular belief, the people who use them are those you can consider "ordinary," and not your stereotypical genius. Most of these experiences discussed you may have already encountered, and I am sure there are more examples that you can think of yourself. Noticing how these examples occur with people you see everyday, there is no reason not to think of yourself as being capable of becoming an elite contributor to the world around you. The decision is yours.

✐ *The Arts*

The arts are always the most fun to talk about because they are all about creativity. Music, dance, drawing, and painting are all examples of the arts. Learning to bring ideas together in the form of a song, image, or performance takes vision and imagination and has a major impact on the social culture and stability of the world. The arts can truly be looked upon as the most underrated of all subjects instructed today.

One aspect of the "real world" that you will soon hear if you had not already is the phrase "thinking outside the box." This is a popular phrase because this mentality is what keeps entrepreneurs and franchises in business. Engineers, musicians, construction workers, politicians, and parents all use this type of thinking because unexpected problems and new challenges in life reveal themselves daily. Computers, automobiles, books, MP3 players, cell phones, commercials, TV shows, and movies all use "outside the box" ideas to create exciting and new experiences for people. Remember that first-day-of-school discussion we had earlier about how excited you were when things were new? When in adulthood, a part of what you will be asked to do using what you have learned in school is creating that sense of "newness" for others. Exercising your ideas when you participate in the arts will help you keep a creative state of mind that will allow you to impact society (social studies), using problem-solving skills (mathematics) and technology (science). Now do you see why I think the arts are underrated? With the arts you can use skills from other subjects too.

WHAT NOW?

✐ *Get Started!*

You may wonder with all this information shared, what are you to do now? Just get started? Short answer—yes. But more importantly, the topics that we just covered show you the kind of information that is available and explains what these subjects can really do for you. Knowing the truth about a topic and how to use it for yourself gives the subject more meaning, don't you think? School can get real boring very quickly when you go to school just to go!

Explore all areas that the school curriculum has to offer and ask questions to teachers and counselors that will better help you understand the material (this is why they are there!). Do not be intimidated by the subject at all. If you choose not to explore the subject more in-depth after meeting the minimum school requirement, make sure it is a choice based on the conclusions you make from knowledgeable sources and your own thought process and not because you are afraid of the subject based on the false perceptions of your peers. Think about rumors you would see spread throughout school that you knew were not true about yourself or someone else. I'm sure you wanted people to hear the truth so that your peers would not get the wrong idea about you. The same idea applies when making judgments about a subject and how it involves the things you like. Be sure to get the truth and do not get the wrong impression of a subject or class based on the rumors of your peers. Remember, this time period is meant to prepare you to make adult decisions. Making decisions based on real facts is the method used by adults to ensure that they are making the best decisions for themselves and those they care about. Soon, you will be next in line to make these decisions and more than capable of surpassing what adults from past generations have accomplished. Why is this? Simply because the information that is being supplied to you at this age was not as readily available to past generations.

Now is the time to take advantage of all the information currently at your disposal so that you can build your personal capability to a level where you can truly be innovative and make changes that affect the world in a positive way. Similar to a computer being downloaded with a ton of memory, or a lawyer building a case for court, in order to prepare yourself to have the impact that you want, it is best to build yourself a great foundation of knowledge that you can build upon both inside and outside of the classroom. Listening to adults (parents, teachers and current leaders) and learning from their achievements and their mistakes (yes, adults make mistakes—lots of them!), you will see what it takes to respond to the needs of others and learn about the truth for yourself.

✎ Listen For What?

Listening is one of the more positive aspects that separate great leaders from great executors. A great executor can do a particular job well. Great executors do a great job in managing tasks. On the other hand, a leader understands what it takes to execute and provides the vision to enable executors to perform. Leaders have a greater influence on how things work because they have what it takes to communicate to the executors what is needed to generate the vision. What makes a leader special is his or her ability to listen and understand what people need. Leaders are creative (skills learned in the arts!) problem solvers (math skills!) who know how to bring ideas together for the benefit of others (science and social studies!). Executors do not have to focus so much on maintaining and building their understanding after they are informed of the task. Since executors are so focused on the task, they cannot make positive changes because they do not understand what people need. As a student, you want to focus on being a leader because the leader is always thinking ahead about what more can be learned so that more changes can be made.

Take for instance classroom teachers. What makes teachers so special is that they understand what it takes to bring out the best in their students so that their students can showcase their creativity in doing things never done before, and better than ever. Teachers actually learn from their students, which makes them become better teachers in the future. This means that both the teachers and students have a learning experience while in the classroom. To put it another way, the teacher is really just the lead student in the classroom! Because the world is constantly changing with new ideas being born everyday, a teacher cannot teach the same way five years from now as he or she did today. The world will have changed too radically! Teachers are great examples of leadership because they look to see where the students' needs are. Through creativity and problem solving, teachers build environments in the classroom that allow students to exercise their own world-changing abilities.

"What now?" is all about taking advantage of your current opportunity to build awareness of the world around you. In doing so, you provide yourself with what you need to make changes to your social environment as you see fit. Neglecting this opportunity places the control of your decisions in someone else's hands, which will give them the ability to make decisions on your behalf. Which do you prefer?

WHAT'S NEXT?

So here we are! We have discussed how as students we can take information and look at it in a way that pertains to what we see and how we think. The motivation to learn and grow academically has reached a whole new plateau for you. Now you are all ready for—what? Exactly! What is next after you have learned all of these skills? You have taken on the challenge of learning how to solve equations, how events and decisions changed history, even how penicillin still seems to be the cure for just about everything (well, almost everything). What next?

Remember how we continue to emphasize the idea of being in control of your own life and making decisions on your own behalf? Now comes that time. After learning the subjects offered by the school systems and building on your knowledge base that allows you to affect change, next come the choices you make to understand what it is that you excel in and have a passion for doing outside of school. Having a strong interest in a subject is important in getting the best out of you in a given job or career outside of school. Music, art, engineering and science, law, construction, and education are all based on the basic ideas that you are learning now. Asking questions based on your curiosity is important in deciding the career you want for yourself. You may even find new occupations (entrepreneurship) based on what you see is needed in society from your own experiences at home or while going to school. The purpose of learning is to apply what you know so that you can make changes in the world for the better. Understand that what is written in books has already been done. The world will always have executors to maintain present discoveries, but more importantly, society needs leaders to take what is being done now to a new level of innovation and discovery. This is where you come in. Understand the "real world" around you and shape your goals and dreams within it. Do not neglect the resources around you and later look to see if you are ready for the "real world." Build these skills within yourself and find out if the "real world" is ready for you. Rest assured, you will be amazed at the outcome.

Reference

Greenspan, B. (1997). *The Olympians' guide to winning the game of life.* Santa Monica, CA: General Publishing Group.

ABOUT THE AUTHOR

Alcott Germany II, is an experienced practitioner when it comes to presenting simple solutions to complex problems. When Alcott shares ideas, he prefers using vivid images and stories that connect with his audience. This approach has resulted in personal and team achievements as an engineer, logistics manager, and Vice President in multiple industries and Fortune 500 companies.

Alcott earned a B.Ch.E. degree from the University of Detroit Mercy and a M.Ed. degree in Curriculum and Instruction from the University of Phoenix. While at the University of Phoenix, Alcott developed a student-centered learning method that enables students to gain knowledge in the classroom through teamwork and active participation. Alcott later used this method to create an online tool to help teachers deliver student-centered learning in their classrooms.

Alcott worked at various companies, such as Lear Corporation, Henkel Surface Technologies, DuPont Automotive, Procter & Gamble, AT&T, BASF, and Rocket Companies during his career. Currently, Alcott serves as owner of Instructional Design Solutions, LLC, a company that focuses on system design, leadership development, and operational excellence for large and small businesses, schools, and non-profit organizations.

For twenty years, Alcott's impact as a respected community leader, student, and teacher has reached various communities, encompassing locations that include Detroit, MI, Southwest Georgia, Atlanta, GA, and Ontario, Canada. He will always have a passion for supporting schools, communities, and innovators through creative design, collaboration, and public speaking.

Printed in the USA
CPSIA information can be obtained
at www.ICGtesting.com
LVHW070547230924
791358LV00021B/44